SCHIRMER'S LIBRARY OF MUSICAL CLASSICS

Wolfgang Amadeus Mozart

Concertos

For the Piano

Critically Revised, Fingered, and
the Orchestral Accompaniments
Arranged for a Second Piano

by FRANZ KULLAK

AND OTHERS

G. SCHIRMER, Inc.

DISTRIBUTED BY

7777 W. Bluemound Rd. P.O. Box 13819 Milwaukee, WI 53213

MOZART. CONCERTO FOR PIANO IN E FLAT MAJOR

PREFACE

The autograph of the score of the E-flat major Concerto is in the Royal Library at Berlin. The parts for the trumpets and drums are added at the close on a separate sheet. Mozart originally conceived the work with simpler instrumentation, and added the above instruments later as a support for the Tutti. Although the manuscript shows some subsequent alterations, in hardly any case is the text doubtful. An occasional uncertainty arises from the circumstance, that Mozart's orthography varies in the notation of accidentals. The sole passage giving cause for serious hesitation is discussed in Note 13 to the first movement.

We collated the score-editions of Richault, André (1853), and Breitkopf & Härtel; the old Breitkopf & Härtel edition of the parts; Pauer's edition with second pianoforte; various new editions; and the arrangement by Hummel.

For the Tutti, and in those passages in the Soli where only the right hand has an independent part, the autograph gives almost without exception the direction "col basso" in the lower staff of the piano-part. Sometimes, instead of this general direction, the notes are written out. Conformably, our text gives, in all such passages in the Soli, the entire bass-part; it is omitted only where Mozart added rests in the cembalo-part; and in coöperation with the modern orchestra it is equally superfluous in the Tutti. The editions with which I am acquainted are frequently inconsistent in their notation of the bass; it is often omitted without reason, and also added now and then where the composer did not require a support for the double-basses.

All heavily engraved slurs, dots and expression-marks are found in the autograph. Interpolations by the editor are recognizable by lighter engraving. _____

My sincerest thanks are due to the librarian, Dr. Kopfermann, and to Dr Erich Prieger, for the MSS. and publications which they so kindly placed at my disposal.

DR. HANS BISCHOFF.

Berlin, 1886.

15780

W. A. Mozart.

CONCERTO
in E flat major
for the Pianoforte.

Composed in Dec., 1785.

(1) In the new Breitkopf & Härtel score-edition, both here and in measure 7, the note g^1 is added in the violin-parts. There is no authority for this note either in the autograph or elsewhere.

15780

Printed in the U. S. A.

(2) In the old Breitkopf & Härtel edition of the piano-part, also in Richault and Hummel, $f^2\sharp$ instead of f^2

15780

6

(3) In the first source mentioned on previous page, and in Hummel, *bb* instead of *b*.
(4) The new Br. & H. score-edition gives *a²b* instead of *a²*. Reinecke the same. The autograph has neither ♮ nor ♭.
Either is possible.

15780

(5) In some editions, the notation of the closing chord is not full; Pauer gives, in the treble staff, only g^1
(6) In the autograph, the staccato of the violins is indicated only in this one place.

(7) Br. & H.'s old edition of the parts, also Richault, Hummel, Peters and Reinecke, mark the chords in the next three measures arpeggio.

(8) In the old Br. & H. edition of the piano-parts, c^1 instead of e^1b.

(9) An earlier, subsequently altered reading of the autograph, is

(10) In the old Br. & H. edition of the piano-parts, also in Richault, and Reinecke, no ♯ before f^2
(11) Slur forgotten in the autograph. The f^1, in the next measure but one, is also omitted.

(12) Frequent reading: ⎰ Analogous variant in next measure.

(13) The abbreviation of this period by two measures is, when compared with the parallel passages, very strik-ing. At this point in the autograph there is a sign and the figure 2. The parts for trumpets and kettledrums, which (as remarked in the Preface) are written out on a separate leaf at the end of the MS., mark 25 measures to be rested, later changed (possibly by the author) to 23. There was doubtless an oversight here, which later received Mozart's sanction; an artistic reason for the variation in question is not apparent, the movement developing here with the same easy breadth as at the beginning. But, for instance, the abbreviation of the period in the first Tutti after the Cadenza in the Finale, must be judged of differently; it is æsthetically justified, as hinting at the close.

(14) The autograph originally had the following reading, later changed by the composer:

(15) In the autograph, f^1 instead of g^1. This is probably due to hasty notation. Many editions have adopted f!

(16) In the old Breitkopf & Härtel edition, also in Richault and Peters, this measure also reads thus:
The tie from d^2 to d^2 is in Richault.

15780

(17) Andre, Pauer, and Peters, give only the note g♭ on the first beat.
15780

Cadenza by J. N. Hummel.

(18) The autograph indicates the interpolation of the Cadenza thus:

N. B. Facilitation:

(1) The tie from e^1 to e^1 is omitted in the autograph; probably merely forgotten. It is not given in the score-editions.

(2) In André and Pauer: ; corrupt reading.

15780

(3) In the old Breitkopf & Härtel edition, also in Richault and Hummel, there is an appoggiatura instead of the trill-sign.
(4) See Note 2.
(5) Text acc. to the Autograph. All other sources read d^3 instead of f^3.

15780

(6) In the Autograph stood, at first, g^2; this was changed later to f^2. Hummel has g^2.
(7) The omission of this tie, in the autograph, is also probably due to an oversight.

(8) See Note 6.
(9) The old Breitkopf & Härtel edition, also Peters and Hummel, give *ab* instead of *bb*.

15780

34

(10) Some editions set the turn-sign over a♮♭.

(11) In several cases the trill is continued only to a♮.

(12) Neither the new Breitkopf & Härtel score nor Reinecke has a turn here.

15780

(1) The printed sources give ties in this measure and the next; they are omitted in the autograph.
(2) A frequent mistake here is a^2 instead of b^2.

15780

(7) In the autograph is a slur between g^2 and bb^2; probably an oversight.

Cadenza by J. N. Hummel.

Andantino cantabile.

(8) Both the old Br. & H. edition and Richault give f^1 instead of e^1b, following a slip of the pen in the autograph.

(9) Several editions give $a\natural\flat$ on the first beat; this is not sanctioned by the direction in the autograph, "col basso."

(10) Orthographical mistake of the autograph in the parts for violins and violas: The same mistake recurs in the old Br. & H. edition of the orchestral parts, and in Richault and André.

Cadenza by J. N. Hummel.

piu cresc. ed accel.

calando e ritard.

Tempo I.

Tempo I. Str.

(11) In the new Br. & H. score, and elsewhere, the rhythm of this measure reads thus:

(12) The old Br. & H. edition, also Reinecke and Peters, give *g-bb* instead of *eb-g*.

(13) In some editions the *bb* is lacking.

(14) Some editions add here, too, a tie between *eb - eb*.

(15) according to Peters, Reinecke, and the old Br. & H. edition.

(16) Earlier reading of the autograph, subsequently altered:

Variant:

(17) According to some editions, the fourth sixteenth-note reads d^3 instead of $e^{3}b$.

(18) Variant, after Peters and Reinecke. Both in Richault and the old Br. & H. edition, the higher part reads as in the variant.

(19) The autograph indicates the interpolation of the Cadenza thus:

Cadenza by J. N. Hummel:

59

15780

(20) Some editions read:

(21) In several editions the basses are incomplete, (incorrect). Here, for example, *d* is often given instead of *e♭*, and three measures later *e♭* instead of *G*.